advance praise for TRANSITIONAL O

"'The shoreline like a boulder,' writes Adrian Silbernagel, 'has the softest skin in the world—you will question yourself.' If a poem is, as John Donne would have it, an argument with God, then the poems in *Transitional Object* evolve the argument into a softer, more considerable inquiry. Silbernagel questions the gestures and betrayals of a beloved through a delicate grammar. He tells us 'mythology has lost its meaning' and uses the ballast of word play, calling his addressee 'nearly beloved' to further draw us into his confusions. The intelligence wrought in *Transitional Object* explains itself through various entanglements, whether that means 'sex-drenched' linens inside a walk-up apartment or is itself a phenomenological rendering: 'when dusk snows its dark / wool down on us,' we understand that the lovers are shackled to so many abandoned objects, alone together, a union apart. Here, we experience the chutzpah and agony of language, their bleeding together a kind of romantic undertaking. Here, I celebrate the self that tells us, 'For I...am mercurial / memoryish.' Memoryish, we are."

NATALIE EILBERT

"Some books create a feeling of gratitude and recognition whose intensity is startling. *Transitional Object* is one of those. Adrian Silbernagel works language like stained glass, making one densely-pigmented, luminous scene after another. If you too have asked 'who this 'I' is that steals and gives,' if you have also told yourself, 'the life of me/requires so many more bodies than this,' you need *Transitional Object*. Let it help you move from one self to another, one moment of being to the next, again and again. It's that important. Silbernagel has 'waded deeper into the rubble' of the structures that oppress, 'where [he] now lie[s] in wait' to welcome you and help you on your way."

JAY BESEMER

"At once a challenge and an invitation, a seduction and a demand, the work collected in *Transitional Object* does what poetry must, and only the best poetry does: it undoes the world as I know it, and remakes it entire. Adrian Silbernagel's utterly original voice, his mastery of language, his perceptual power, do no less than de- and reconstruct reality. These poems both employ and interrogate the power of word, image, and symbol to say what we mean; they question, and ultimately restore the reader's faith in, the possibility of making meaning at all. If all this sounds abstract, the poems themselves are anything but—these are muscular, embodied, deeply sensate works, alive with the passions of being, rich with both the tensions and wisdom of body and mind. Silbernagel is an important new voice, and his vision is one that we have not yet seen, nor will we see again soon."

MARYA HORNBACHER

"'If to be mirrored was your motive, / it was mutual; if to last forever, mutual.' Adrian Silbernagel's *Transitional Object* offers a means by which to both shatter and make solid, to create 'me' in flux, to write 'I want my voice to explode in my dream without waking me,' when a metonymic 'planetarium blasts apart inside me' or oracles as object. Light bends the object that talks to itself as if a lover, as kind or unkind. It nurses the edge, 'contemplating not death, but the conditions of resurrection,' knowing that metaphors don't die, we outgrow them. At times light is a bully to the hypothermic, who 'gives way to heat, or the illusion of heat.' But as the heat casts off metaphysical skin or, if it dissects itself, turns inside out, it adds that 'the animal in motion stays aysmmetrical.' As it devises material 'threadwaste, threshold' through the condition of the body, it puns, the double having its way with the language because 'mythology has lost its meaning.' Meaning is a monster stared down and eaten with 'the beat and what falls between the beat.' Even if each piece of shatter resurrects as an animate fantasia of broom splinters. 'Do not ask: what shall we make of all the disappearing furniture?' Instead ask what becomes you, an epic figure that might be believed in as the 'names for each turn light takes as it enters a sanctuary: lux...lumen...illumination...' Between the maker and the made, the poem is written to this you who is a hole and wholes and holy, that 'for the life of me / requires so many more bodies than this.'"

M.J. GETTE

TRANSITIONAL OBJECT

[poems]

ADRIAN SILBERNAGEL

the operating system
print//document

TRANSITIONAL OBJECT

ISBN: 978-1-946031-51-8
Library of Congress CIP Number: 2019939288
copyright © 2019 by Adrian Silbernagel
Interior edited and designed by ELÆ [Lynne DeSilva-Johnson]

For additional questions regarding reproduction, quotation, or to request a pdf for review contact operator@theoperatingsystem.org

This text was set in Edit Undo Line BRK, Minion, Freight Sans, and OCR-A Standard.

Cover art and design by ELÆ created using *in vivo* time lapse images of sensory neurons affected by insect hormone in drisophila.

Your donation makes our publications, platform and programs possible! We <3 You.
http://theoperatingsystem.org/subscribe-join/

the operating system
www.theoperatingsystem.org
operator@theoperatingsystem.org

TRANSITIONAL OBJECT

[poems]

2019 OS SYSTEM OPERATORS

CREATIVE DIRECTOR/FOUNDER/MANAGING EDITOR: ELÆ [Lynne DeSilva-Johnson]
DEPUTY EDITOR: Peter Milne Greiner
CONTRIBUTING EDITOR, EX-SPEC-PO: Kenning JP Garcia
CONTRIBUTING EDITOR, FIELD NOTES: Adrian Silbernagel
CONTRIBUTING EDITOR, IN CORPORE SANO: Amanda Glassman
DIGITAL CHAPBOOKS / POETRY MONTH COORDINATOR: Robert Bałun
TYPOGRAPHY WRANGLER / DEVELOPMENT COORDINATOR: Zoe Guttenplan
OPERATIONS, BROOKLYN OFFICE: Joe Cosmo Cogen
SOCIAL SYSTEMS / HEALING TECH: Curtis Emery
CONTRIBUTING EDITOR, GLOSSARIUM: Ashkan Eslami Fard
CONTRIBUTING ED. GLOSSARIUM / RESOURCE COORDINATOR: Bahaar Ahsan
DESIGN ASSISTANTS: Lori Anderson Moseman, Orchid Tierney, Michael Flatt

VOLUNTEERS and/or ADVISORS: Anna Winham, Adra Raine, Alexis Quinlan, Clarinda Mac Low, Bill Considine, Careen Shannon, Joanna C. Valente, L. Ann Wheeler, Erick Sáenz, Knar Gavin, Sarah Rosenthal, Richard Lucyshyn, Amanda Huyhn, Charlie Stern, Audrey Gascho, Michel Bauwens, Christopher Woodrell, Liz Maxwell, Margaret Rhee, Lydia X. Y. Brown, Lauren Blodgett, Semir Chouabi, J. Lester Feder, Margaretha Haughwout, Alexandra Juhasz, Caits Meissner, Mehdi Navid, Hoa Nguyen, Margaret Randall, Benjamin Wiessner

The Operating System is a member of the **Radical Open Access Collective**, a community of scholar-led, not-for-profit presses, journals and other open access projects. Now consisting of 40 members, we promote a progressive vision for open publishing in the humanities and social sciences.

Learn more at: http://radicaloa.disruptivemedia.org.uk/about/

Thank you to the following journals, in which selected poems from this work originally appeared:

The Atlas Review
"Species Dysphoria"

The Columbia Review
"Étant donnés"

Cosmonauts Avenue
"Standing the Test of Time (A How-To Guide)"

The Destroyer
"Time-Lapse Resolution" "Conditions of Resurrection"

ditch;
"Tranquility / Modern World Landscape" (published as "Necessity / Tranquility")

E-ratio
"Teen Angst / Grand Theft Auto" "Love Song / Suicide Bomb"

Fruita Pulp
"Cables" "Fair Verona"

JuxtaProse Literary Magazine
"Visual Fatalism" "Causa Sui"

>kill author
"Thrownness"

Ouroboros Review
"Subject to Change" (published as "Your Euphrates")

Painted Bride Quarterly
"Understatement"

Radioactive Moat
"Unstatistically Speaking" "Uncertainty Principle"

Requited Journal
"Antonyms for Reticence"

Rufous City Review
"Lux Continua"

Thirteen Myna Birds
"Faminism" "Autocorrect"

Two Hawks Quarterly
"The Scapegoat"

TYPO Magazine
"Vorticism"

CONTENTS

3. WHO YOU ARE WHEN NO ONE IS LOOKING

4. ON LOVING THAT WHICH YOU CAN BARELY RECOGNIZE

NOTES

I. NOTES ON INDIVIDUATION

Where water slurs around the edge of the delta's mouth,
and celestial North is not "someplace else" but a continuation
of the river—calf, thigh, spooning the shoreline like a boulder
has the softest skin in the world—you will question yourself.

Think back to a time when everything we touched could turn us
into a palace—like Midas, only it was you who became
the glistening walls for a world of subjects to meander, maybe
admire, maybe lose themselves in the ambrosial architecture

of your body. A time when metamorphosis was your first response
to a warm wrist, a curious glance, the earliest hint of human
suffering. And how somewhere down the gold-coloured line
that bounds, uninhibited, from "this mystical garden" to "that

dark creature lurking in the corner," and back to you—a stunning
light show—mythology lost its meaning. Admiration became
demeaning. A collection of mason jars filled with the Missouri
means *I don't want to lose you, but still I can't trust you*

to stay. Inside me, where a body of water and sky is disjointed,
you are a boulder I can't encompass. If we believed in myths,
and I were a palace, you'd walk through me; maybe burn
your place in the celestial array of invaders, and leavers,

and I'd go to the river—a streak of suffering
light—and empty the jars at the knees
of an unbroken world.

BUNDLE THEORY / INFINITE SCROLL

Your first night alone overseas,
plagued with jet lag and transparency—
Your fumbling transaction with the terse bank teller
and programmed flirtation with a helpful bystander—
Those hijacked plans to see the Orsay and the Louvre
before *crashing in the evening and dreaming of you*—
Your virgin taste in relations "unconditional"
and affinity for exotic affairs that would follow—
All those clever artists who promised you an in—
All your deadnames nailed to the wall of a museum—
An amphibious existence that supports itself accordingly—
suspended, with class, between erasure and a rat race—
On your marks—*Where*—get set—*do I go*—
The interventions you insisted were *unfair* and *premature*—
Your postcards slipping through an aging woman's fingers
while elsewhere your life continues to un-scroll—
Chicago, Seattle, book deal, funeral—
Those girls you only wrote because they made you
feel invincible—Those boys you only wrote
because you wanted them to swoon—Your Sartre,
your Pinot, your eventual tomb—Your relapse
sponsored by foreign cash and the words
Closing soon, whoever you are,
find what you look for.

To those whom the gods would undo, they said the truth
was *gnarled but glowing like embers embedded in the ground.*
How unseen, the old view, how crude and indescribable—
the vast bay window costing NASA an arm and a leg
—*to see what they could see.* Up north, there are more dark days

than ways through them, a thick skull buckling in the cold
-blooded riverbed, a winded depressive who'd kill
to pay rent, the indiscriminate expansion of everything
under the Sun—all becomes one / who could have been
an astronaut. *The unearned wonder, the succor, the loss.*

I'm convinced that we were—all of us—fireflies
in previous lives, and while the blue faded, the filament
hung on. *But not until we're buried are we bulbs.*
Redundant: don't think of wings as obsolete, but *novelty*—
whose roots bloom black and bottled messages

read: *Save me from myself…* To those whom the gods
would burn out, they lent flame, and watched
panoramic cliques corrupt the wicks of troubled teens.
Think Da Vinci's first angel, think Descartes' wax
-strewn gown. To these delicates, we dedicate: *threadwaste, threshold.*

*And who do you propose may have pressured the free
object's fall?* Thus mocked the anchor tied tightly
to the anchoress, tossing and turning down the path
to enlightenment: *Dream your way back through the valley
of the shadow, mind the weather, remember who you are.*

A mythological figure, come hell or high water, full circle or color.
The hook that would catch your attention, reader. The link
"appearing broken" in a chain of events, viz., an outstretched hand
on the suicide bridge. *The moral man would serve, he put to words.*
A kid again: bearing an eraser at the point of no return.

THROWNNESS

The night sky: a voluptuous black
swan taking a bullet to the breast / bloody blossoms

blooming all at once upon a time
-lapse photograph *See with your eyes*

not with your hands evokes the fondest
of the fond: my brother, my god

complex examining the pavement
for a smooth patch, shooter for blemishes.

I walk through the valley of your shadow:
a slim chance weighed down

with just enough marbles
to drown me and just pretty enough

to impress the other Pisces at the show
and tell display of adolescence

whence we carry, timidly, timidly,
our half-formed senses of self.

We lose touch for different reasons
from diametrically opposed coasts. For me

every hangover's aurora borealis
is charged with telepathic electrodes

transmitting felt warnings at speeds
I hesitate to translate. For you I appear

dying in too many dreams; over too many rivers
I waver, never casting that first stone.

The agate moon hanging dull and low
among the fireworks, then retreating

into some remote corner of the lake: far
more well-rounded than I'll ever be.

A thousand rock stars smashing their guitars
on a dark stage: sparks cascading down

upon a sea of fans, a surf wave, me
taking it all serious and in.

Temporary centerpiece. Bomb threat
apocalypse theory-head. Beast of Water

cusping Aquarius She who hates
because she knows not what she is.

Amphibian. Second born second sex
addict par excellence Sister of the boy

who cried Keeper of the cat-eyes I've been
called lots of things in my life.

FAMINISM

Once resilience was all that could be said
for the terrain: once the lewd wind
took the living breath out of the geese:
the laughter and the wings out of the wind:
once fallen: the wobbling V stood

for unidentifiable: aerial voyeurs
and their 8mm bird hearts
set on Deep South / gone degraded
in the soil. Such crises.
Such maggotry of cornfields

turned us all anorexic: shriven
at the cutting edge of August.
Just amateur Cowboys trading
glances with premature Indians
when the mayor got on the radio:

Gonna hafta make a maze out of this—
and you swore by that broadcast
you'd have me for your own before fall did
drown our little war songs
'neath a blanket white as God

and the Good Land dreamed crooked
dreams of what could have been
flammable. Carnival tickets
left over from the last church
bazaar, our little fading

souvenirs. Your hat my saving face.
What had been our wilderness

destiny manifesting
fifty-cent admission fees for hours
of sharp turns, you crushing

on the shy, dark-eyed neighbor
girls who'd give in—given
we were all afraid of worms
that summer, and of getting burned
once we called off the war.

TEEN ANGST / GRAND THEFT AUTO

It all started with you wanting
to set off all the alarms without a thought
to how selfish that crime-
to-criminal-ratio would've sounded.
I tugged at my ski mask and swore
to play superfluous. Perhaps I was praying
for all the wrong things, teased the world
in all its mock-oyster glory. Underground
subways converted into anti-rain dance halls
—the beat and what falls between the beat—
Ginsberg, Ferlinghetti, fanatics passing out
-dated literature out to ravers at the tunnel's mouth
exacting a dripping pulp. Water torture
was all in our heads, like the song
you only loved because it made you feel invincible
as it boomed from your new used snow-white
Corsica—bass cranked, heart pounding,
eyes close as they'd ever been to sleep.
Dream-screams flee lips crimson-kissed
by all the pricks you made out with
like a thief in a jewelry store, delinquent
written all over her car, and I'm total
-ly that pearl right now.

Drop your weapons, she says. I say I don't have any. *You're lying*, she says.
I say *Jesus, I'm sorry*. My story so simple I'm ashamed.

*

At eighteen you rose, threw on your flannel and snuck out
with your wicked step dad's pistol, and some plans.

*

Homicide or suicide, everyone asked, except me.

*

"Come As You Are" was the party theme.
I came alone. My dad thinks it's a stage.

*

There was the question of how to present ourselves, distinctions
between butch and femme, blood and let-blood, between love

And letting love, to be made. There was the issue of the pseudonym.
All I asked was for your name. You laughed, said *pending*. I said *Jesus, I'm sorry*.

*

Simple, he'd say, *it's just a stage*.

*

Then the show got ludicrous, the lead singer smashing his twelve string
on the amp: cataract of sparks like red stars.

You asked if I was taken, but then the party crowded in like the blind
around the miracle performer, like fans around a flame.

*

Homicide or suicide, they ask. I hide.

*

Don't forget you're taken, said my boyfriend as he drew
a dozen roses from behind his back and handed them to me

before he vanished into twilight, and I changed.
"Come As You Are" was the party theme.

*

I came in his flannel.

*

My bouquet, blocks back: a copula, a cataract of red
petals spilling from the bridge rail to the river down below

The lead, smashing his twelve string on the speaker:
explosion of distortion and petal-red stars

*

My sternum, a double bass pedal beating triple time
Homicide, you lied

*

But then the lead got ludicrous and flew off
the stage into a sea of fans, a surf wave, my bouquet

Still littering the bridge blocks back, your bullets
still poisoning the river, as we came

*

As we were.

As to what or who will deliver you to day:
decide to climb a fire escape.
No emergency emerges—climb it anyway

and as you mount the final rung lean back
to open and flood your lungs with onyx
oxygen: elixir of the half-gods of dawn—

even overdose. It is of paramount importance,
here, to not fear abundance: the full
moon fondling a harem of androgynous birches

at the outskirts of town—femme on femme
light—white magic just *cast*
across the lost field of vision

like no tomorrow, and *oh*—the deep breeze
moaning through those smooth,
those moon-strewn knees.

It is of paramount importance to embrace
repetition, again and again,
the object of passion, and let go—

the breath gaining speed for speed's sake,
no—for the sake of the breath—
a wind chime unfreezing from the frost

-bitten branch—relearning how to sing
is not rocket science, nor life support,
whether art or not art, think of the infinite

masterworks eight appendages can muster
in the hours of entanglement
when 9-5's dissolve into the ambiance

of ambulances and neon and late-night cafes
become quarantines and safe
houses and purgatories for Johns and Janes,

Janes and Janes, leaning into one another
with their backs to the window,
beyond which the Great Outdoors

grows numb to us all. See how
their hands dance together, without rings.
To slow aging, think, and be

warmed for a little, and fall back,
subtracting from the world
the persistent lack of snow angels.

I am the keeper of the heights, wind-tender and wild-eyed. Alpha and Omega, Beginning and End, I Am the cast and the chorus and the audience all at once: meaning lonesome. A limestone castle crumbles with my every exhalation; whenever I inhale a little color leaves the world, my children, listen— to the hypnotic pull of the full moon pregnant with every sad poem ever written, the willow and the terrible truth the wind has to tell it—and tell me who I am. If you refuse: sleep will come like a thief, the lover, set sail in the tossing and turning; your bed frame become ladder become kindling is no fire escape. I am the top of the world and the sea, now evaporating. You who I carved out of an eyesore, you sight for sore eyes, rise: walk bravely in circles to the music. Do not ask: "What shall we make of all the disappearing furniture?" Think only on those things that must be discovered, that may never be created nor destroyed. Dreams come to those who ask for much but need little: a sound tonic, a fistful of sand. Ye wing-bent, ye with no way down, take comfort: you aren't the first, and are far from the last.

LOVE SONG / SUICIDE BOMB

As the insomniac dreads the night, so does the city
grow petrified of being what it is, needing what it needs.
Take the bridges we managed, despite downpour and detour, to let burn.
An animal in motion stays asymmetrical: this was me trying to get even
with history—carbon footprints all the way down.
The metropolized skyline like a girl, by definition, interrupted
by the politics of entrance, essence askance, warship lands
her one-hundred-story deal: published, perished.
They're tightening the border now, punctuating things without thinking
what they might be killing off. *If this is freedom, I'll have no part in it.*
If this is scandal, I want in on it all. In Times Square, a figure ate
dirt, background ate figure, a skating rink falls asleep full
of fractured bones, New York City full of terror,
and I still can't remember where I parked that night
for the life of me / requires so many more bodies than this.

If my methods were juvenile, yours
were all blood, cum & conquer.

If I was camouflaged, you were camoufleur.
If muse-starved, I was scarcely in your favor.

If to be mirrored was your motive,
it was mutual; if to last forever, mutual.

If downtown there is still a muraled stairwell
that leads to two doors: one deadbolted, the other

hoarded over—I got everything I asked for.
Despite delusions of grandeur. Despite the night

& day difference between underground
& sellout, invincible & adult.

If there was one thing I asked for,
it was not to be seen & not heard.

If I was dreadlocked or angst-filled,
moon-pale or ethereal, you were adamant:

I was doomed to unravel. If memory serves,
you said as much that night by the river

gone swollen with snowmelt, gone viral
from trying to level with the trestle, that night

when your camera caught my wandering eye & made
my mind derail: my string of conditionals cascading

graffiti & all into your stone-cold waters, your glass gaze,
your brick wall. If your light-hungry world turned

me rabid, turned me pixilated;
if "a picture speaks a thousand words"

is a truism another, keener poet already had
his way with—say *the apparition*

of these faces in the crowd, say *petals,*
on a wet, black bough—there was nothing left to steal.

2. SACRILEGE IS THE NEW SECURITY BLANKET

This much is given: a set of organs, an infinite set of needs.

Be wary of those who fear intimacy: who privilege their need
to be taken seriously over their need to be taken, full stop.

This much you'll take with you to the grave: heart, lens, certain neurons.

The severity of whose nightmares can be measured
in slips of the tongue, at dawn or in broad daylight.

With these you will walk through the valley of decisions,
making shadows of which you are terrified, despite having made them.

Whose offspring—petals on a wet, black bough—are conceived
in underground subways that read "save me from myself—"

Three times you'll deny having made them. Thus your migraines
will multiply, your labor pains, grow thrice-excruciating.

Whose pictures omit a thousand words; who turn a blind eye
toward Jerusalem, a blind eye inward.

Your pupils will forever be at war with your mind: threatening to flood it and, by turns, to cut
it off from the light source.

Who view the heart as, not a four-leaf clover, but a compass rose:
its direction not discovered but forever self-imposed.

Your guilt you will braid into a noose for lack
of better instincts, for lack of forgetfulness.

Who deny that, in cell years, seven is the turnover rate:
after which it's anyone's guess who's counting.

Between the needs of the body—and the virtues of the mind—fall the upright—forever lost
in translation— Cyan coins of dusk rushed through your chest as you fell to the East / *as I*
fell to the West—

My spine shone, and you promised to make me shine
brighter than any known star, laser, or halo.

What was I supposed to say? How was I supposed to age?
I'm no human, and god knows you're no angel.

Do what you will, I said, and I'll go where I go.
Cut my umbilical cord. Commit me to the flames.

I.

I steal things I'm too ashamed to borrow:
the hours at the end of your day
you inhabit so gracefully; your glance, that place

where electromagnetic waves go
entangled, go to war. My independence deteriorates
with my optical fibers; fireworks

seizure on the nerve-screen and I mean,
if you need to make nothing out of something
you should say it to my face.

Was our love not handcuffs; was what held us together
not your hate-dread of the other
racing pulses I've felt fluttering inside me?

I let them all get away
and was sentenced to the page, which for a time
at least gave my crimes meaning.

II.

The things I steal I rarely savor: her body forms
a lump on my retina as my brain
leaves the restaurant. *I'm afraid of what my hunger will do.*

At some point the cones must take sides:
If blue is heaven, red is solitude.
A tension builds that will inevitably be broken

between the understanding and its object.
A shudder grows that must be released
between the shoulders as the spirit remembers

why the Gothic architect Suger had a name
for each turn light takes as it enters a sanctuary:
Lux when it pours unimpeded from the sun,

Lumen when it streams through stained windows,
Illumination when it fills the believer.
Remembers what it was, but couldn't stay.

III.

Call the memory of color sublime: call it despair.
The lover comes and goes like a recurring nightmare
where the face goes white, the eyes swollen,

the soles of the feet slice open on the boulders
when the tide rolls in—comes and
goes between trial and error, *I do* and *do us part*.

If I were trapped in a cathedral on this darkest night
of the drought and cried out to The God,
I doubt he would hear me. When I was the cruel word

scrawled across sandpaper, strapped to a missile at 30,000 feet,
you were cactus limbs strewn around my shelter
in the nuclear fallout. When my name became Tantalus,

I made you my rain stick: shaved glass tumbling through
thorns turned inward: a secret storm
no light could enter, without first breaking thee.

Wings fold back and break off in unbearable winds.
Neither of us had the luxury of watching
my plane leave insofar as you crashed once I said goodbye come dawn
and I was stuck inside it. Love, to be honest
is to board a metal bird full of strangers all moving
in the same general direction at terrifying speeds
much as a train of thoughts throttles across a page, meaning anything
you think you want—oxygen mask, suicide bomb—can and will be
held against you. Boundaries blur, book drowns, as watercolor aircraft spirals
bright lights down below may belong to several cities or simply a home
once christened fluorescent, now taken by flame.

TIME-LAPSE RESOLUTION

I want to be in love and of it, to live
in a postwar, radioactive city
or on a ship at the bottom of the ocean
because I'm just that invincible, my force field's just that bomb.
I want to know God, to approach him
with no puns intended, with a gun to my head,
to be beside myself, outside myself,
to crave the unspeakable—I want my voice to
explode in my dream without waking me and when
the alarm clock goes off on the horizon
I want my body to lie prostrate as my fake one
runs through strange streets soaked with blood and maybe gasoline,
and Flame, I want that rush to the head
of butterflies foretelling our impending destruction
and subsequent mass production of hate mail
and frantic prayers for halos—I want to be in danger of believing
everything they tell me, of taking the prophet on the subway
for a terrorist, religion for protection, quantum entanglement for proof
it's not just me and my decisions. I want to believe
every word of it—and laugh. I want my life back.

What our nature is / can't be captured: this I know.
On black and white film, elements may appear interchangeable.
The flames were like ocean spray—a surf wave—we could not see through them.
At the end of this world will rain hourglass. Will time pass like light. Will light separate
the shards from the sand as we wade deeper in. A gray sun may hang
in the background, disinherited. Understand: a great lens encompasseth us.
Understand: some may lose their faith. Camera now turned on / the Light of the Dharma:
his face soft as lotus petals, firm body. An arrow called Gravity points away
from an unnamed center, Beethoven's *Moonlight Sonata* playing from a foreign car
crouched beside the curb, upstream a boy anoints the monk's head with gasoline.
There are two kinds of people in this universe. *Minstrels, drag your rigid bows across*
the trembling cello. Reporter releases the shutter / shudders: a flourish of orange
flags and yes a few blue even—*In my lungs, an unspoken manifesto*
now combusting— Did he stay in that pose, and for how many centuries:
These questions can't be answered simultaneously—and will burn—

CONDITIONS OF RESURRECTION

I've been shut up
for millennia in this ward
with a terrible question
on my tongue, I've been
reticent stricken and bound
by insomnia because
dream-language smacks
of drunk slurs and I've
had my fill of those. Believe me
when I say that heaven is this
world, and this world is
a theater where paupers go
to don themselves splendid
and render hope possible,
because we're all just
deus ex machinas taking turns
 with the suspension cables.
Believe me when I say that
I know that beauty is in
the noose through which
the gaze shoots its arrow
accidentally hitting a sparrow
flying crooked against the wind
a split second before
your foot slips. But it's more

than that, and less: it's the dark
figure penduluming under
the meteor shower / between
two Judas trees. See, I'm attempting
to explain how I know that feeling
is the kick-away foundation
of belief, but on good days
belief is a paper boat that sets sail
in a gentle stream, in hopes
of disintegrating before it
reaches the waterfall.
All I'm asking is why this is
a bad thing. Why when dandelions
disseminate
I'm filled with a dread
that could move mountains,
the very mountains
through which my brothers
and sisters are tunneling
their way toward the light.
Why nothing, absolutely nothing
is so complicated as that silence
that bewitches the mind
just prior to creation, or so simple
as the one that follows
the end of the world. Because god knows
we're addicted to these intervals,
and for this, like god, we'll be judged.
But like god the author

is not sorry and offers
no explanation as to why
my poems give rise to more
eyebrows than jihads,
and dares whomsoever
has never sat down to write
a letter to the universe
and couldn't find the words,
who's never strapped a bomb
to their person just to feel it
detonate, and spent the rest
of their life at the river's edge
alone, contemplating
not death, but the conditions
of resurrection—
to cast the first stone.

Tell me what you breathe again, and why we're so different
as to not contract the same types of virus or commit
the same hypergraphic slips of the pen:
You're right—I left. Strange logic I keep
between these hemispheres, queer equator
into which collapse my wildest fantasies
of decadent crystal chandeliers crashing
down on the End Of The World
Party table, where eating is as futile as trying to reason
with your ex. Rays of light
stream from a clichéd, an abused
source of energy we failed to keep interested
or interesting. The last time we spoke, it was over
a pop song that the DJ hadn't heard
had gone endangered, and I'll never forget
the way you looked at me, as if I was the Sun,
as if to say *tell me what will happen when you're gone,*
when what rules the world has no use
for my scent or for my lungs.

AUTOCORRECT

The letter I said fell out
of my pocket on my way to deliver it
didn't. What kind of joke is this?
The one where you want
the whole package, but not the whole
truth and nothing but the truth,
and therefore, I adore you.
Agenda-centric, metaphysically insecure,
I pretend for all practical purposes
this world will last forever—
send you bottle rocket
bouquets to trick my cliché-dar.
My cobweb shimmers
you make believe desire
your firefly wings.
Rows of xo's put to shame
my purple prose: a planetarium
blasts apart inside me.
You see, what you don't see
you don't need to know.
(We're all whores putting out
applications for halos.)
Whoa—woe is me.
How easy it must be,
to throw away a hole
–punch ceiling.
Stencil wreckage
everywhere moonlit,
coddle it in bulk
like there's no tomorrow
even though there is.

Nearly dry: a lone rose descending headfirst from a piece of twine, double-tied.
In absence of Atropos, we are partners in infinite crime.

We are gathered here with the window open, on cold linoleum creaking.
Through voodoo blinds the Christian neighbors peeking. *When she flew her airplane into me*

it all felt so inevitable: the burns on my wrists, her taste in my mouth,
the burns on my ankles. How in my last life I was hanged

and how I was hanged the life prior. How we tried and tried.
I don't know what to feel anymore, save for the wholly ghostly echo of petals coming

down hard, coming down singular, all around the kitchen table.
My voice, a bomb trapped inside a blazing elevator, fails

and fails to combust. Father, forgive us. Demons, evacuate. Nearly Beloved,
take my oxygen mask—I've said my vows already.

ANTONYMS FOR RETICENCE

Having breathed the invisible glass,
having forfeited my gas mask: last chance
before the sea levels everything
in its way—killing it with contrast—

to cough up an excuse, a vow, a word for how
eyes are still the vulnerable vowels
through which slip a soul: sound fury burning salt and me
not getting any of it down. The un-crying shame

of a beached whale bathed in wailing gulls,
little Sally selling seashells by the sea-corpse
in the dream where I lost my voice
screaming: *Has anyone seen this pearl?*

Lines cast out from tired poems and tied to limestones
too fragile to make a dent in anything,
get wasted on this window,
shattered on that heart.

If broken, call me a liar. If bleeding, call me Ishmael.
If god's blade dulls, if gunmetal blue rivers
never lap crimson forth, would not even Moses slit his
to prove the Nile sentient?

Where is the grain of truth in these fool's gold waves—
these days that find you waiting on the Furies
to sweep down and disperse
your silver lining into acid-black dusk?

When they come, you set the island on fire
with your glory-torch: a fist-full of words,
my photo cloned and posted
all across the flaming hillside—I saw it

with my own eyes, and only my own eyes
know how many oil spills I counted on
that quiet drive, which, because circle, felt endless.
Feelings are toxic or they're nothing

and I'm banking on the former and I'm drowning
on the shore. If some secrets aren't lies,
if confessions can be true,
I'd slay I'd for you.

NIGHT OF FAITH

I don't know what it means, that there are means by which days
age gracefully: with the wherewithal of shadows on the wall

of a home, where our better halves wade through broken
bottles to mend a broken whole, where storm clouds stop dyeing

their roots dark, gain composure, and smaller stars starve
themselves to breath out of the corners of our eyes. I don't know why

these pieces of us must perpetually pass through shafts of light like
lost astronauts: in and out of fame, now and posthumously—

3. WHO ARE YOU WHEN NO ONE IS LOOKING

Tender summer. Sunburned and salted. Gypsy-hearted.
Drank us like a vampire, fed us like a mother, smothered us like a lover
the night before she has to leave for war. Summer of protect and keep,
cherish and savor. Of lavish gifts and live sea burials, of flushed necks
draped in perspiration pearls. Summer of dry heat and dangerous cocktails,
of hot lust and flash floods and gulls lost in cloud cover, of dark, sex-drenched linens
gone damp and cool by morning. Summer of take, and give recklessly. Of bourbon
and lemons, tomato and avocado sandwiches. Of rotting secrets and private avalanches:
your bed overflowing with my tears every color of the rainbow. Summer of blindsided,
of helpless, of swept. Of shipwrecked before scurvy could set in. Summer of heaving chests,
vows and threats, of why are we doing this. Summer of infinite, unfathomable riches
spent somewhere between past and future, desert isle and leaking hull. Summer of waiting
to be told where the soul's weather comes from, what it means, and where it goes.

DEAR ENEMY EFFECT

You implore me not to talk about your past
until we learn how to sleep again.

My word these days is mostly filler, is only maybe
ten percent substance, like the bouquet your grandmother carried

so carefully up the aisle during the drought.
You curse the wind for throwing things, for raising its voice;

the clouds for looking so macabre and melodramatic. I promise to try
to be less like the clouds and the wind. I want to say that

we need the rain, but I worry you'll use it to hide from me
your liquid humanness, to appear distant and stonefaced, like the god

your mother cursed when your father left her
gasping for air between his pickup and the garage door

like the petal pressed between the pages of her own mother's bible,
the only gift she received the day that she exchanged her freedom

for a roof and some walls. I'm afraid our dispositions are new testaments
to the same old laws, to the same old character flaws:

you mock everything that weeps; I distrust everything that walks
into the mirage of me and immediately begins drowning.

We are cherry blossoms caught. / Inside the static loop of loss.
The lack of color in our fingers suggests a common manner

of gripping the things we carry / let carry us: this pen, this bottle,
this hand that I hold as I lay awake wondering

where you go when you dream, and this hand you hold
as you go wherever it is you go.

I need to know exactly where my voice went, when it left me.
I need to know exactly what happened that night
when the moon dripped ominous stalactites
down the walls of my insomnia boat,
when you stopped answering my phone calls
and didn't come home until morning light bled
through broken glass and ruined blinds, smearing your skin
and clothes with unfamiliar shadows. I need to know why
you agreed to leave the bar with him, where my imagination
could at least get its bearings, could talk me down
from the nauseating thought of that n^{th} story window.
Did he even have real furniture, or was his bed multifunctional
like mine was back when we first met, when I used to take you
back to my studio apartment and fuck you until dawn
because you refused to fall asleep next to anyone
you didn't trust completely? Exactly how far back
did you follow him into his cave? I begged you to break
that black box down for me and build me an explanation
I could live in. But every time you added a brick, the structure shifted
and my eyes filled with terror, and my eyes fill with rage
each time you took a brick away. When I could no longer stand

to look at you or speak, you laid down your spade,
hung your head, and walked off into the sunset.
For days, for weeks, I tried to follow your lead,
but if to forgive is divine, to be human is to live in search of truths
the acquisition of which would destroy you. I waded
deeper into the rubble, where now I lie in wait.

It's staircase simple, addition-and-subtraction simple.
Simple as what you ate for breakfast, or what you did last evening:
dry toast and black coffee, a drink at the bar with a friend—a well drink, single.
As an ounce of gin, six of tonic—or one of rum and six of coke; as going Dutch
then going home alone. It's as simple as I have a partner, as we're trying
to build a life together out of the remnants of broken bottles and broken trust.
Isn't it magnificent. Isn't it something. It's as simple as it's complicated
and quite frankly you have no business asking. Simple, like the freshly-cut,
freshly-sanded-wood scent climbing up the front of this old apartment complex:
sometimes refusing to stop at the main entrance, sometimes staying
in your hair and clothes all the way home.

PRISONER'S DILEMMA

We move under the cover of night, three months before our lease ends. You want no housewarming party
to remind us of our elsewhere, our whence. I agree to pretend that we've lived here for all eternity—
here with the slanted floors and perplexing floor plan, the light switches we still can't locate
after all these eons. I agree to pretend our story is not a filthy sponge that we had to twist and twist.
Gobs of cardboard boxes threaten our coherency, as do our skewed circadian rhythms.
Oblong folds of paper-thin skin might mean sleep, depending on the presence of a pulse I can't check
at this distance. I lie awake wondering if I'm the cause of your vacant condition,
and if not, who is; if there's any song vile, any violin small enough, to do my pain, my greed, and my jealousy
all justice; if any second we'll come to our senses, and have to break the lease again.
It kills you when I talk this way, and I come to my own defense. I didn't mean to upset you, I say.
I just wanted to make sure you're human, and show you that I am. I wring my hands
and remind myself to believe what I said.

Our faces are screen savers. My favorite flavor
is tobacco on an empty stomach; yours is bit-tongue blood.

We've mastered the art of inaudible temper tantrums.
We've learned and forgotten how to love

that to which we've grown accustomed.
Burnt leaves spill from my fingertips

onto the porch you swept this morning
while I slept off my hangover, where I live off

the Camel Crushes I bum, and the glances I steal
from pretty strangers. You shredded all the evidence

for or against your own unfaithfulness,
used it as packing foam. Every box I open

is another can of worms; it takes everything
I have not to kneel down and comb through the mess

of orphan syllables with my bare hands.
Soon that mess will have touched all my things,

and it will take everything I have not to leave.

THE SCAPEGOAT

I carry my vows
on my tongue so that I'll choke
before I break one. Such sudden,
episodic deaths you've come to accept
as a fact of your life now, just as you've
accepted as facts my incurable sorrow
and my need to make and make
-believe. You know that I can't help it
if the light from my computer screen
interrupts your REM cycle, if the cold
sweats I wake in you must also
wake in, if my dream city is populated
with doppelgangers of your exes
-turned-assassins I was born to obliterate.
You buy me camouflage pajamas
and a lucid dreaming instruction manual.
In the morning, you help me rinse
the blood from my hair and dragon wings,
just like you promised. I want to come
clean about fudging the death count
and dragging you into this worst of all
possible nightmares, but something deep
inside of me stutters, and just in time
the bough breaks.

I've got some questions I need answered; you've got some answers you don't need questioned.
I've got some time on my hands, and the things I used to fill it with have started to rub me the wrong way:
your hair on my face, a cat o' nine tails; your breath on my neck, a damp fog that crawls
into my clothes, my bones, and falls asleep; my poems, ores covered in a bloody pulp, a serrated serenade.
And I wonder to how many sea-faring monsters a single word can refer before it stops meaning anything,
who this "I" is that steals and gives, slays and prays for mercy, that left its fingerprints down another's spine
last night, before feeding it to the five-thousand-headed dragon in its dream. Most of all I wonder
where my book went, and how many teeth you've been lying through lately.

NIGHT OF INFINITE RESIGNATION

As our treasure sunk, I silvered: white locks spilling like light
through arthritic fingers looped through rusty shears.

Our closure was the quiet convergence of shadows
on a hull's wall, was the autistic acoustics of water

Poring over chainmail: *Come closer* and *I promise*
not to ask what you've done with my letters / with my last

One hundred years. Was through the dead air and empty space
that the spear cannot pierce, that I passed, finally—

Remember that time I knocked your antique hourglass
off the mantle, how the heaps of sand scattered
like ant hills when I fell, how one minute I was drunk
and on top of the world and the next minute the world was on top
of me saying, "What are you doing taking comfort in this spinning ceiling
fan keeping the bedroom cool and the electric bill low,
these lavender waves lapping against your chin, this bottle, this home
you won't even fight for anymore, my big bronze Buddha sitting in lotus pose
staving off the Sandman and the Loch Ness Monster, my matchless staying power."
You said matchless, you did not say infinite. I felt so lonesome and godless
you turned off the faucet and cleaned up the mess so I wouldn't have to
dwell in it. The excruciating divisibility of that time piece. Each stray grain
standing for a fraction of a fraction of that week that lost me
all I wanted and left you on your knees, wondering what you'd missed.
I bet if I looked close enough, I could still see the pale silt gist of it
glistening in the floorboards, the way grease glistens
in the cracks of a clock maker's hands.

AND SUDDENLY IT MAKES SENSE WHY NOTHING MAKES SENSE

Every day you'd wake and look
for proof that not everything repeats itself,
that some things happen exactly once:

the shapes of the ice crystals collecting on our eyelashes,
the extinction of a species,
solemn vows, the whole Holocene,

the idea of the first stained glass dome ever built
and the way each sinner felt as those colored rays entered
their pupils as they passed through the cathedral,

or the way I felt the morning
I stood in the front yard and you stood in the doorway
and asked where I was going, as if you didn't know,

as if your decision to give up everything for me
and my decision to leave you
were not like two designs at the end of two kaleidoscopes:

two finite sets of tiny panes we rearranged
until blue in the face. If only I could have seen
what only you could have seen: that part of me that was ready

to die off and give way to belief in us, or faith at least,
as hypothermia gives way to heat,
or the illusion of heat.

4. ON LOVING THAT WHICH YOU CAN BARELY RECOGNIZE

ÉTANT DONNÉS

In a deep closet locked from within and lit
by a single gas lamp, I am building a bed of twigs
and a landscape with a waterfall

out of the materials you've been leaving on my doorstep
for the last two decades: a lump of pigskin,
a bundle of sticks, a bolt of velvet.

My wartime rations, you called them.
For the last two decades you've been leaving me,
little by little, to my own devices: a withered bouquet,

a shrinking wardrobe, a fistful of word-sand.
Piecemeal, I rescind my commitments
to the outside world. My bastard boxcar children

roam the streets of one hundred different cities, shore up
in bottles on one hundred distant coasts
in one hundred strangers' poems. In deep shame

in the deep shade of a Saguaro, I am daydreaming
of hydroplaning, of a threshold, of a home
-wrecker's body. A black box cracks open in the desert sun,

and from it spills a naked woman you don't recognize,
even though you've met her hundreds of times,
her pale skin covered with petals

from the flowers you brought me, the pine needles you picked
with your bare hands. I fall to your feet
and offer up my best explanation, my fattest lamb.

TO FATHER TIME AND MOTHER CERTAINTY

My poems unfold androgynous as nightmares from neurons / anorexics from slumber /

dandelion seeds from stems clutched tight until REM sleep loosens clenched fists—

airy asterisks attempting to accelerate the transition from Life of Lies to Honest Death

—and though none of this is glamorous, you're convinced I'm convinced that it is.

This title you've worked for, this game you've perfected, this secret club you're a part of

isn't sexy—it's sick. Soon you'll ascertain my sexuality is an extension of my eating

disorder / is an extension of the chronic confusion you are somehow responsible for.

No small wonder my only conviction is that convictions are shoelaces and chronicles

are straightjackets, and I'd rather go barefoot and insane than let you dress me again.

What's wrong with your old clothes? You're such a pretty girl—such a pretty little

girl-ghost in all of these photographs. Only Aslan has ever heard me speak of that

wardrobe and knows how I go mute with a feeling I can't name each time I open

a birthday card listing off all the things you wish for me, like *that you'd remember*

your roots and answer our calls once in awhile. Because if memory serves, unruly weeds

had no place at your table, "queer" had no place in your vocabulary, and children

who refused to be seen and not heard had not earned their transparency, or your respect.

I come from a long line of photophobes. No Fabios.
Call me pre-transition MTF, or Most Taunted Fugitive.
Call me Amish, Old Fashioned, call me Crazy
Horse hiding in a cornfield as white man
stalks the prairie with his camera stealing
soul-emissions off of the steaming beasts. Zoom
in on whatever suits you, then crop out the rest of me.
Call me the widower of the queer, quiet painter
who died trying to capture the brazen dysfunction of skies shot up
with artificial light, with just three pigments, some water and a good mind
to burn down every movie theater from here to Frankfurt, Germany.
Call me Pink Triangle Prisoner 11067, formerly known as *Liebling*.
Call me superstitious by choice, paranoid by necessity,
alive by default. Feel free, call me out.

WRONG BODY OWNER'S MANUAL

Try to remove your things from their graves without waking them. Do not ask
"what will we eat?" and "what will we wear?" See there, a blanket belonging to a girl
who'd been thrice-starved: once by a God, twice by her own volition. Take it: it shall serve as your cape.
And here, a little doll head, attached to a feeding tube now dangling freely from her lips
will bring you luck on your journey. You threw a match into these fields once, now raise it: build a fan with your lungs.
Her hills will rage and her trees will orange as your vital gusts blow through them. This is not voodoo: this is tough
love: there is no anesthesia. There is a red flag flickering off in the distance, meaning "peril." Take it
to mean "free association." Run past the police with your mouth on fire and follow the crowd
of surgeons down to the sea-hell where the youth are trading seashells for aloe and the mermaids are singing
each to each. Steal from them according to your ability. Sing with them according to your need.

Lessen, voluptuous feathers.
Fold up fanwise, hide
behind your sisters, single
file now. That pipedream
you insist on parading
does not become you.
That crystal castle unfolding through
the smoke from the ground
-fire in the path of your exile
does not become you.
These desks, these bus seats,
these pews are all reserved;
you best stand idly by. Over there
is a reservoir of know-how
for you to dip your feet into. Well,
why are you just standing there?
Don't you have anything prudent
to wear or practical to do?
Shame on you and your abuse
of confessionals and shrink
booths. This "I" you fancy
as mountain water rioting
into the watershed, has this "I"

been Pope-blessed? Has it
fathomed the ten thousand things
that could happen to a girl
en route from Chiapas
to El Paso, from this bar
to your apartment? Are you sure
you don't want a ride?
What's wrong, aren't you
noose-shy? Are you not scared
to die? Here, let me help
you get a little more bang
for your buck. Let daddy
help you into those handcuffs.
Does yr man purse like that?
Does yr wallet like living
off my tips, dyke? Are you sure
you can make it to the border
by midnight, pumpkin?
Don't forget who bought you
that nice glass slipper
you walked away from.
Is your skill set even marketable?
In fifty years will your feet still feel
like waiting tables?
What if your knees go
brittle with age and can't
genuflect? What god will
want you then?

My dream-self's guilt is cello-heavy. I carry it with me
everywhere I go, so that it doesn't smother her when she sleeps.
When I lie down at night, she wakes and relieves me of the load. I float
to the ceiling and watch her stumble underneath its dead weight
with the gusto of an ant. When she cries out for help, I wake
and take the load back again. She floats to the ceiling smiling down on me
a sad, grateful smile that fades when her eyes close. I can't bring myself
to tell her that I dropped it once, many years ago, and that it's never sounded
the same way since. When her eyes close, I set the beat-up instrument down
on the ground and crawl back into bed. Yo Yo Ma plays Bach's *Sarabande*
on my stereo as I fade in and out, flirting with sleep. I don't tell her
who it is that's playing. She believes what she wants to believe.

GLOWING IN THE DARK IS NOT A SUPERPOWER

But something we do daily. By "day" I mean only the shrinking doily
of light through which a whole black hole must squeeze before our eyes
can adjust, before the dream seamstress drifts off at the wheel
before blowing out the candle, before the child in the sky can cut stars
from the singed scraps of cloth he salvaged from the burn pile.
Love of my life, cause of my insomnia, sometimes when dusk snows its dark
wool down on us, I search your face for the sheep you counted
as lost, and wonder if I'm one of them. But I still take comfort in the night's small
certainties: the tiny movements muscles make when the rest of the body lies paralyzed
with dread; that I'd wake, here, again, for the last time; that you can love something
and still shake its soot from your feet. Restore to meaning the plastic asterisks on which
I wished my adolescent life away. Don't pass over. Lie me to sleep.

MAY MY LOVE BE LIKENED TO GUERRILLA ART OR OPEN COMMUNION

My invisible inner indigo child
lets their little plastic soldiers go
out at high tide and swim
in the disassembling moats
of abandoned sandcastles. So what
if they take relish in the wreckage,
perpetual scandal of landscapes
giving themselves over after everything
we did for them. After twenty years' servitude
to a jealous ghost, I'm done searching
for the perfect words to ask your forgiveness
for the times I stood shivering in a bed sheet
on the shore, as the wafer moon turned blood orange
and pulled you out to sea. To say that I need you
to remember me in neon and concrete,
all gumption and centrifugal force,
my trench coat pockets full of flasks
of Merlot and cans of spray paint, our bodies
darting in and out of dark alleyways
that long, and long after we're gone
will explode into color.

VISUAL FATALISM

Late summer, kite weather,
muscles remembering the day you took

my hand in the wheat field: nautilus of fingers
to which the shrinking diamond was tethered

unraveling open. Once, you shared my awe
of the transcendent, of what goes beyond

flesh and blood, overflows silo and water tower,
makes fully grown men fall apart. Our Father

learned from his father, who learned from his father
how to corset a season, how to wrangle golden waves of grain

in barbed wire, how to pray for rain and discipline us wild oats:
me and my unnatural questions; you, his only begotten son.

The last time we spoke, you were letting me know I'd done enough,
said you'd found him in the prairie during a thunderstorm

lying face-down on a hay bale, his limp arms stretched out
around it—territorial almost. You gathered his heavy body

was a dead metaphor, said *please don't shoot the messenger,*
said *this family is that bale of hay, and you are the lightning.*

A crack in the truth window exposes a wall's sod interior
to moisture, to empty nest syndrome. Late summer,

kite weather, still no olive branch. Whatever brother
I had is gone, has left me for harvest. Untethered

in a wheat field, I let go of kite string after kite string;
dissolve into vertigo, into golden waves of grief.

You dreamed me down the railroad tracks
that wrap around
your hometown like a holster belt.

You recalled slingshots, forgot bruises,
recalled scarecrows,
forgot coming out to them.

My brothers didn't call me
Houdini for nothing, you said.
I took the right rail; you borrowed the left.

Our hands met in the middle:
formed a knot that swung
back and forth above the ballast.

If it was up to your ego, I'd say
we were the last two girls left standing
in a game of red rover,

boldly beckoning the neighborhood bully
over. If it was up to your conscience,
you'd let me choose a more honest metaphor.

We balance-beamed past piles of leaves
in which bricks lie buried, past windows
in which pillow fights go south

and malevolent, and coal-filled
stockings hang heavy from the mantle
all year long. Your gaze stayed lost

in the vanishing point. The knot grew
clammy-cold. You recalled consequences,
forgot antecedents, forgot doubt,

recalled crucifixes, recalled shame,
forgot to give me a face.
I didn't see the plume of feathers

billow up from the plum tree; didn't hear
the birds' wrecked hymn
or the whistle's shrill falsetto,

your breath's blade sharpening, aghast
against the lump in your throat.
If it was up to your neck, it was your anger,

your paralysis, it was the smoke and fire
and brimstone through which
a younger soul might have made its escape.

But you did not wake up. You tightened
the knot. You would not let go,
not even for my sake.

Sometimes, once the lights in the hall
have gone out & all is sterile

save for the half-frozen hummingbird
in my ribcage & the police cars

carving solemn couplets
into clean, white streets I steal

a glimpse of my raccoon face,
then my whole gross body

in your eyes: the only mirrors I'm
allowed near these days.

It happens suddenly,
the way most wanted

fugitives are caught, how a cot
or bed is overcome with something akin

to dread & begins trembling
when a train's whistle cuts through the dark

cocoon of drug-induced sleep.
There's no telling if I'm shrinking

or backing away or standing still as the walls
grow up around me, as words are now

more dangerous than numbers are
more dangerous than sharp

objects used to be. It's not enough,
I say. I say they still need

to grow faster, to border
on cancerous. For I am

a shrewd lab rat, am sex gone
wrong gone totemic, am mercurial,

memoryish. In this single life I've managed
to prey & be prayed on, femmely

& forcefed, butch & broke
& fixed. We have been over

this. No part of me must go unharnessed,
or if it does, I must trust you

would never let that part of me up
& run rampant. I must trust your solid

sternness the way a younger sister
trusts her elders to dress her

down when she doubts or daydreams
about silk undergarments,

or worse, men's clothing. I can't pass
through solids, but I'm pretty

certain that if there are things that can,
I evolved from those things,

or from the things that broke down
into them. Radioactive materials, say,

or the queer little prince the royal family had
buried at sea. I need to believe this arrangement

is strictly necessary; that however many
shecells I claw through I'll emerge

in a warm room wherein you are patiently
waiting, for worse & in sickness.

The motes around my reflection
will have never looked so deep,

so much like my mother's as you count
out the pills that help me pass

the night more easily. Leave me be,
I'll say, but we'll both know that I can't

mean that, & so you'll stay,
& so I'll stay.

NOTES:

VORTICISM

"The apparition of these faces in a crowd; / Petals on a wet, black bough."
is from Ezra Pound's poem, "In a Station of the Metro."

CREATION STORY

"Cyan coins of dusk rushed through your chest as you fell to the East / as I fell to
the West" is an adaptation of a line
from Tessa Rumsey's poem, "The Stranger."

STANDING THE TEST OF TIME (A HOW-TO GUIDE)

"Mountain water rioting into the watershed"
is from Tessa Rumsey's poem, "Fantasy Coat."

DEAR ENEMY EFFECT

"We are cherry blossoms caught. / Inside the static loop of loss" is from Tessa
Rumsey's poem, "April Fools."

Greetings comrade! Thank you for talking to us about your process today! Can you introduce yourself, in a way that you would choose?

My name is Adrian (he/him/his). I'm a queer, trans poet.

Why are you a poet/writer/artist? And: when did you decide you were a poet/writer/artist (and/or: do you feel comfortable calling yourself a poet/writer/artist, what other titles or affiliations do you prefer/feel are more accurate)?

Poetry, to me, is radically autonomous speech. It is autonomous because it cannot be paraphrased. It speaks for itself. Nothing and no one else can speak a poem's meaning for it, not even its author. Poetry is also critical, in that it troubles linguistic convention, and the habits of thought and language that structure and condition our experience of the world. Furthermore, poetry elevates and illuminates everyday words, objects, thoughts, and feelings so that they can be seen and felt in a new, different, and sometimes powerful way. I'm a poet because I can't imagine any other way of being / striving to be.

I have been writing creatively, and writing poetry, as far back as I can remember. As a kid I wrote stories, poems, letters. As a teenager, my poetry practice became a means of exploring and articulating thoughts and feelings I didn't feel like I was allowed to speak about. It feels most natural to call myself a poet because poetry has been the most consistent and stable organizing force in my life and person, more so than any other belief system, community, identitary label, or interest. No matter what else I've done or been or been about, my commitment to poetry (while this relationship has evolved) has been unwavering. "Devotion" is a good way to describe my relationship to it.

What's a "poet" (or "writer" or "artist") anyway? What do you see as your cultural and social role (in the literary / artistic / creative community and beyond)?

I guess I'm kind of an agnostic with respect to the "purpose" of art. At times I feel like I can kind get behind Adorno's notion of "autonomous art": art that invites critical reflection and introspection, that rejects the posture of passive consumerism, that asks to be read slowly and on its own terms. The saying "no ethical consumption under capitalism" applies to art as well, and in the current political and economic climate, and in the age of social media and the infinite scroll, art and the conditions required to achieve and/or appreciate it become the mark of privilege. Because art takes time, and time is money, most of us are lucky if we can "afford" a serious creative practice, to say nothing of opportunities to get our work out into the world. Every artist has a unique set of circumstances (privileges and personal or systemic barriers) that they're creating within. Right now I am in a good enough place, emotionally and materially, to have a fairly consistent writing practice. This is a huge privilege. During the first few years of my transition, however, job, housing, and financial insecurity coupled with the social and emotional implications of transitioning in a place like Lexington, Kentucky, put a halt to my creative practice. It was the longest break from writing I've ever taken, lasting about three years. The last poem in *Transitional Object*, " Species Dysphoria," was actually the last poem I wrote before beginning my transition. After that I was too busy fighting off panic attacks, self-medicating, and trying to keep a roof over my head to even think about poetry.

Accessibility is an issue in publishing just like in healthcare. Why are certain people groups more prolific (or published or widely read) than others? The same reason why certain groups have longer lifespans and lower risk of ailments than others: because they don't face the same institutional barriers. So maybe art is kind of the cultural equivalent of a blood pressure cuff. It gauges and monitors the health or vitality of a society/culture, the individuals and groups and institutions and power structures that comprise it.

Talk about the process or instinct to move these poems (or your work in general) as independent entities into a body of work. How and why did this happen? Have you had this intention for a while? What encouraged and/or confounded this (or a book, in general) coming together? Was it a struggle?

I am constantly on the lookout for links, repeating images or metaphors, contiguous layers between poems that might suggest a greater unity. I could probably guess where (or which part of my upbringing) this teleological impulse comes from. Hah. As for *Transitional Object* in particular, it didn't occur to me until late in the game (after the poems in the manuscript were already written) that I had a book. I had been operating on the assumption that the earlier poems in the book belonged together, while the later poems (despite being in a dialogue with the earlier ones, and despite both groups of poems being obsessed with the same questions and ideas) belonged to a separate work, given that their speaker was now a different person, with different beliefs, values, desires, different ways of thinking and speaking about their person and relationships and experiences.

I was still on my "break" from poetry, and deep in the throes of early transition, when it occurred to me that the impulse to quarantine the earlier poems from the later in this way originated from an idea of selfhood (as a stable or "reliable" narrative subject whose identity, desires, core beliefs and values endure through time) that didn't arise from, or correspond with, my own journey as a queer trans person. My story, my person, is, at least by all appearances, fragmented, discontinuous, a multiplicity of selves that exist in relationship with one another and with Others. So why should my book and its speaker be any different?

Did you envision this collection as a collection or understand your process as writing or making specifically around a theme while the poems themselves were being written / the work was being made? How or how not?

I've never had success writing about (or even writing around) a predetermined subject or theme. Most of my poems start with a single line (which often gets cut during revisions) and I discover the poem as I write. Similarly, it's always during the writing and editing processes that links or connections to other poems emerge.

What formal structures or other constrictive practices (if any) do you use in the creation of your work? Have certain teachers or instructive environments, or readings/writings/work of other creative people informed the way you work/write?

In the formative stages of a particular poem, I try to write, as often as I can, in one-to-three-hours sessions. These time restrictions, while somewhat arbitrary, provide a balance of structure and play that's conducive, for me, to writing poetry. In the editing stage, I'll just edit until I feel like I'm running up against burnout. At that point I step away, and stay away until I'm able to come back with fresh eyes and a less codependent attitude.

As far as influences, there are countless writers, thinkers, and artists who have influenced my work in one way or another. This list is by no means exhaustive, and the names are listed in no particular order: Theodor Adorno, Judith Butler, Helene Cixous, Chogyam Trungpa, Lucie Brock-Broido, Tessa Rumsey, Marina Tsvetaeva, Rainer Maria Rilke, T.S. Eliot, Friedrich Nietzsche, Soren Kierkegaard, Antonin Artaud, Bas Jan Ader, Marya Hornbacher, M.J. Gette, Jay Besemer, Elæ [Lynne desilva Johnson], Daniel Reetz, Aaron Asphar.

Speaking of monikers, what does your title represent? How was it generated? Talk about the way you titled the book, and how your process of naming (individual pieces, sections, etc) influences you and/or colors your work specifically.

Deciding on a book title was one of the most difficult and frustrating parts of the whole process. I went through several, initially landing on "On The Origin of Species." This title pointed to the themes of evolution, differentiation, and hence personal identity byway of metaphor (speciation as individuation), but ultimately I decided, after some nudging from the brilliant M.J. Gette, that this Darwinian title wasn't really continuous with the book's imagery and symbolism, which draws more on psychology/ psychoanalysis than on biology/natural science. So while evolution in a biological sense is certainly present as a layer of the work, it's not the book's central idea either. There was something else, too, that the Darwinian title was lacking, which I'd eventually realize was the book's relational dimension: that push and pull of self and other, I and thou, that animates the poems. But at the time, "On The Origin of Species" was the closest I could get. It was months before the title "Transitional Object" came to me. I was in a therapy session, and the therapist mentioned something about transitional objects: objects that children identify with and assign meaning to in times of change, or in the absence of a parent or other important Other, and it just clicked.

What does this particular work represent to you as indicative of your method/creative practice? your history? your mission/intentions/hopes/plans?

First and foremost, this book represents, for me, my commitment to poetry: the choice to write poem after poem after poem, with no guarantee that said poems will turn out, much less culminate in a book. It represents the hours and days and weeks and months and sacrifices and solitude that the writing life entails.

Secondly, because *Transitional Object* loosely documents a decade of experiences that culminated in the decision to transition, a decision I came to after the last poem in the book was written, it quite literally represents a previous life (or lives), a previous self's (or previous selves') journey to the threshold of that decision.

What does this book DO (as much as what it says or contains)?

The structure of *Transitional Object* mirrors traditional narratives. At first glance, the book is a coming-of-age story told through poems. However, coming-of-age stories presuppose a numerically identical self that persists from time x to time y, a notion that the speaker can't quite buy, much less live up to. So the book calls forth these assumptions, only to call them into question. As the speaker struggles for definition or commitment, from the beloved or the world or their own person, they illustrate the deeply relational nature of the self, a fact that the speaker both mourns and relishes in. The poems mirror this struggle; they engage with and interrogate one another with the toughness, adaptability, resourcefulness, and self-compassion that, for me, are the definition of queerness.

What would be the best possible outcome for this book? What might it do in the world, and how will its presence as an object facilitate your creative role in your community and beyond? What are your hopes for this book, and for your practice?

In my mind, the best possible outcome would be for *Transitional Object* to find readers, even a single reader, who would read it from beginning to end, and upon arriving at the end, feel compelled to read it again. And upon re-reading, would think harder and more critically and more compassionately about themselves, past and present.

Let's talk a little bit about the role of poetics and creative community in social activism. I'd be curious to hear some thoughts on the challenges we face in speaking and publishing across lines of race, age, privilege, social/ cultural background, and sexuality within the community, vs. the dangers of remaining and producing in isolated "silos."

As a white, able-bodied trans man who comes from a middle class upbringing, I have a duty to recognize my privilege and wield that privilege for good, whenever I can. I have a duty to never stop learning, to search out my biases and apologize for my mistakes. The danger of "remaining and producing in isolated 'silos'" is that in so doing we lose sight of our own and each other's intersectionality, each other's particular humanness.

Is there anything else we should have asked, or that you want to share?

I guess you could have asked what I do for a living! I manage a coffee shop in Louisville that is part of a local coffee shop chain and roaster called Heine Brothers'. Not only do we make great coffee, we also do a lot to give back to the community. I'm lucky to love—and be super proud of—my day job!

ABOUT THE AUTHOR

ADRIAN SILBERNAGEL is a queer, trans poet. He grew up in a small town near Fargo, North Dakota, and considers North Dakota home. He earned a Master's degree in philosophy from Texas Tech University before moving to Kentucky. Right now he lives with his partner and two cats in Louisville, where he manages a coffee shop, works on poems, and occasionally travels to other parts of Kentucky to give talks on trans issues and on his experience as a trans man. Adrian is a contributing editor at The Operating System, where he coordinates a web series on creative process called Field Notes. His work has been published in *The Columbia Review, The Atlas Review, TYPO, PANK, Painted Bride Quarterly, Cosmonauts Avenue, Fruita Pulp*, and elsewhere.

The Operating System uses the language "print document" to differentiate from the book-object as part of our mission to distinguish the act of documentation-in-book-FORM from the act of publishing as a backwards-facing replication of the book's agentive *role* as it may have appeared the last several centuries of its history. Ultimately, I approach the book as TECHNOLOGY: one of a variety of printed documents (in this case, bound) that humans have invented and in turn used to archive and disseminate ideas, beliefs, stories, and other evidence of production.

Ownership and use of printing presses and access to (or restriction of printed materials) has long been a site of struggle, related in many ways to revolutionary activity and the fight for civil rights and free speech all over the world. While (in many countries) the contemporary quotidian landscape has indeed drastically shifted in its access to platforms for sharing information and in the widespread ability to "publish" digitally, even with extremely limited resources, the importance of publication on physical media has not diminished. In fact, this may be the most critical time in recent history for activist groups, artists, and others to insist upon learning, establishing, and encouraging personal and community documentation practices. Hear me out.

With The OS's print endeavors I wanted to open up a conversation about this: the ultimately radical, transgressive act of creating PRINT /DOCUMENTATION in the digital age. It's a question of the archive, and of history: who gets to tell the story, and what evidence of our life, our behaviors, our experiences are we leaving behind? We can know little to nothing about the future into which we're leaving an unprecedentedly digital document trail — but we can be assured that publications, government agencies, museums, schools, and other institutional powers that be will continue to leave BOTH a digital and print version of their production for the official record. Will we?

As a (rogue) anthropologist and long time academic, I can easily pull up many accounts about how lives, behaviors, experiences — how THE STORY of a time or place — was pieced together using the deep study of correspondence, notebooks, and other physical documents which are no longer the norm in many lives and practices. As we move our creative behaviors towards digital note taking, and even audio and video, what can we predict about future technology that is in any way assuring that our stories will be accurately told – or told at all? How will we leave these things for the record?

In these documents we say:
WE WERE HERE, WE EXISTED, WE HAVE A DIFFERENT STORY

- Elæ [Lynne DeSilva-Johnson], Founder/Creative Director
THE OPERATING SYSTEM, Brooklyn NY 2018

RECENT & FORTHCOMING FULL LENGTH OS PRINT:: DOCUMENTS and PROJECTS, 2018-19

2019

Y - Lori Anderson Moseman
Ark Hive-Marthe Reed
I Made for You a New Machine and All it Does is Hope - Richard Lucyshyn
Illusory Borders-Heidi Reszies
Collaborative Precarity Bodyhacking Work-Book and Resource Guide - Elæ, Cory Tamler, Stormy Budwig
A Year of Misreading the Wildcats - Orchid Tierney
We Are Never The Victims - Timothy DuWhite
Of Color: Poets' Ways of Making | An Anthology of Essays on Transformative Poetics -
        Amanda Galvan Huynh & Luisa A. Igloria, Editors
The Suitcase Tree - Filip Marinovich
In Corpore Sano: Creative Practice and the Challenged* Body - Elæ [Lynne DeSilva-Johnson] & Amanda Glassman, Eds.

KIN(D)* TEXTS AND PROJECTS

A Bony Framework for the Tangible Universe-D. Allen
Opera on TV-James Brunton
Hall of Waters-Berry Grass
Transitional Object-Adrian Silbernagel

GLOSSARIUM: UNSILENCED TEXTS AND TRANSLATIONS

Śnienie / Dreaming - Marta Zelwan, (Poland, trans. Victoria Miluch)
Alparegho: Pareil-À-Rien / Alparegho, Like Nothing Else - Hélène Sanguinetti (France, trans. Ann Cefola)
High Tide Of The Eyes - Bijan Elahi (Farsi-English/dual-language)
        trans. Rebecca Ruth Gould and Kayvan Tahmasebian
In the Drying Shed of Souls: Poetry from Cuba's Generation Zero
        Katherine Hedeen and Víctor Rodríguez Núñez, translators/editors
Street Gloss - Brent Armendinger with translations for Alejandro Méndez, Mercedes Roffé, Fabián Casas, Diana
        Bellessi, and Néstor Perlongher (Argentina)
Operation on a Malignant Body - Sergio Loo (Mexico, trans. Will Stockton)
Are There Copper Pipes in Heaven - Katrin Ottarsdóttir
        (Faroe Islands, trans. Matthew Landrum)

An Absence So Great and Spontaneous It Is Evidence of Light - Anne Gorrick
The Book of Everyday Instruction - Chloë Bass
Executive Orders Vol. II - a collaboration with the Organism for Poetic Research
One More Revolution - Andrea Mazzariello
Chlorosis - Michael Flatt and Derrick Mund
Sussuros a Mi Padre - Erick Sáenz
Abandoners - Lesley Ann Wheeler
Jazzercise is a Language - Gabriel Ojeda-Sague
Born Again - Ivy Johnson
Attendance - Rocío Carlos and Rachel McLeod Kaminer
Singing for Nothing - Wally Swist
Walking Away From Explosions in Slow Motion - Gregory Crosby
Field Guide to Autobiography - Melissa Eleftherion

KIN(D)* TEXTS AND PROJECTS

Sharing Plastic - Blake Neme
The Ways of the Monster - Jay Besemer

GLOSSARIUM: UNSILENCED TEXTS AND TRANSLATIONS

The Book of Sounds - Mehdi Navid (Farsi dual language, trans. Tina Rahimi
Kawsay: The Flame of the Jungle - María Vázquez Valdez (Mexico, trans. Margaret Randall)
Return Trip / Viaje Al Regreso - Israel Dominguez; (Cuba, trans. Margaret Randall)

for our full catalog please visit:
https://squareup.com/store/the-operating-system/

*deeply discounted Book of the Month and Chapbook Series subscriptions
are a great way to support the OS's projects and publications!*
sign up at: http://www.theoperatingsystem.org/subscribe-join/

DOC U MENT
/däkyəmənt/

First meant "instruction" or "evidence," whether written or not.

noun - a piece of written, printed, or electronic matter that
provides information or evidence
or that serves as an official record
verb - record (something) in written, photographic, or other form
synonyms - paper - deed - record - writing - act - instrument

[*Middle English, precept, from Old French, from Latin documentum,
example, proof, from docre, to teach; see dek- in Indo-European
roots.*

Who is responsible for the manufacture of value?

Based on what supercilious ontology have we landed in a space where we vie against
other creative people in vain pursuit of the fleeting credibilities of the scarcity economy, rather than
freely collaborating and sharing openly with each other in ecstatic celebration of MAKING?

While we understand and acknowledge the economic pressures and fear-mongering that threatens to
dominate and crush the creative impulse, we also believe that
now more than ever we have the tools to relinquish agency via cooperative means,
fueled by the fires of the Open Source Movement.

**Looking out across the invisible vistas of that rhizomatic parallel country we can begin to see
our community beyond constraints, in the place where intention meets
resilient, proactive, collaborative organization.**

Here is a document born of that belief, sown purely of imagination and will.
When we document we assert. We print to make real, to reify our being there.
When we do so with mindful intention to address our process, to open our work to others,
to create beauty in words in space, to respect and acknowledge
the strength of the page we now hold physical, a thing in our hand.
We remind ourselves that, like Dorothy: *we had the power all along, my dears.*

THE PRINT! DOCUMENT SERIES
is a project of
the trouble with bartleby
in collaboration with
the operating system